STUNTS, TIPS, AND TRICKS!

IS

10 9 8

D1056658

Book design by Julia Sabbagh and Cheung Tai

Scholastic Inc.

CONTENTS

What Is Fingerboarding? 4

Get to Know Your Tech Deck! 6

Fingerboarding Basics:

    Standard Finger Position 8

    Starting to Ride 10

Ramps and Obstacles 12

Using Your Ramp 14

Design Your Own Deck 16

Basic Tricks 18

    Shuvit 20

    Pop Shuvit 22

    Ollie 26

    Nollie 32

    Manual 36

Intermediate Tricks 38

Kickflip 40

Heelflip 44

Slides 46

Boardslide 47

Tailslide 50

Grinds 52

50/50 Grind 53

Advanced Tricks 56

Varial Kickflip 58

360 Flip 60

WHAT IS FINGERBOARDING?

Fingerboarding is basically miniature skateboarding! With your Tech Deck and two fingers, you can skate around and perform the same killer tricks as skateboarders do, just on a smaller scale.

In fact, fingerboarding is a sport in its own right. There are serious competitions with prizes— as well as friendly meetup events—all over the country and the world!

GO PRO!

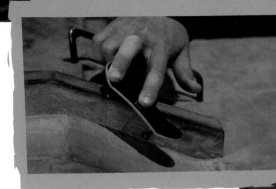

This guidebook will help you learn how to use your board and will teach you a variety of tricks, from the basics to some advanced moves. As you practice and build your skills, you'll be shredding sick tricks like the pros in no time!

Once you know a few moves, the world is your skate park! Like real street skating, you can earn respect by taking on new obstacles with your Tech Deck and creating lines that have never been seen before.

GET TO KNOW YOUR TECH DECK!

NOSE—the front end of the board, which kicks upward. (Note: The tail and nose are interchangeable on a Tech Deck!)

WHEELS—they're how the board moves forward! The wheels are connected to the trucks.

DECK—the board itself, which the trucks and grip tape are attached to.

TRUCKS—the T-shaped metal pieces mounted to the underside of the board. They keep the wheels connected.

GRIP TAPE—gritty tape on the top of the deck, which gives riders better traction and control.

TAIL—the back end of the board, which kicks upward. (Note: The tail and nose are interchangeable on a Tech Deck!)

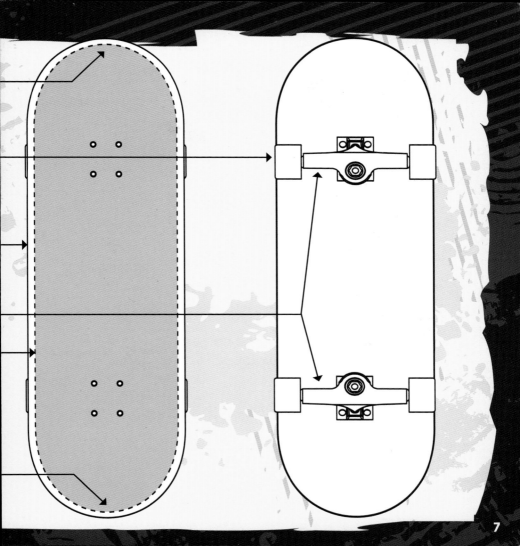

FINGERBOARDING
BASICS

Standard Finger Position

This is the standard hand position for fingerboarding, which you'll need for almost every move and trick in this book.

Place your index finger in the center of board and your middle finger on the tail (the back end of the board).

That's it!
Now let's shred!

Starting to Ride

On a smooth surface, with your hand in the standard fingerboarding position, practice pushing the board forward in a straight line.

Turning Left and Right

To turn while you're moving, push your index finger in the direction you want the board to move. Push your index finger toward the right to turn the board right, or push it to the left to turn the board left. Practice rolling the board around on a flat surface.

Then test out shifting your weight and the exact positioning of your fingers to find what works best for you. Once you feel comfortable riding, you can start learning some killer tricks! (Head to page 18 to dive in to detailed instructions on how to do tricks!)

RAMPS AND OBSTACLES

Use ramps and obstacles to create your own awesome fingerboarding course! You can jump over small household items like pencils or a sticky-note pad or shred on Tech Deck rails and half-pipes. There are tons of ways to work on your skills and nail some killer tricks!

Kicker ramp

Stairs

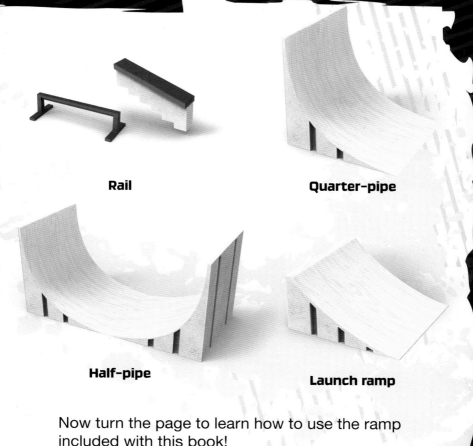

Rail

Quarter-pipe

Half-pipe

Launch ramp

Now turn the page to learn how to use the ramp included with this book!

USING YOUR RAMP

Along with your very own Tech Deck, this book comes with a ramp! You can attach it to the back of this book, or use it on any flat surface. Put it together—then let's get ready to roll!

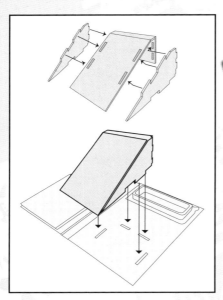

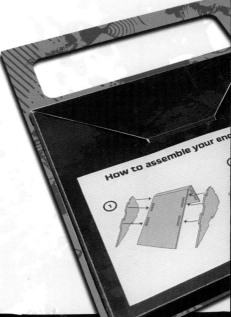

How to assemble your en[d]

DESIGN YOUR
OWN DECK

Just like on a skateboard, the bottom of a Tech Deck is a place for your style to shine! Using their decks as canvases, skaters through the years have expressed themselves by creating original art or customizing existing art with paint or stickers.

How would you decorate the bottom of your board? Use these pictures of blank decks to draw, color, and create some custom designs!

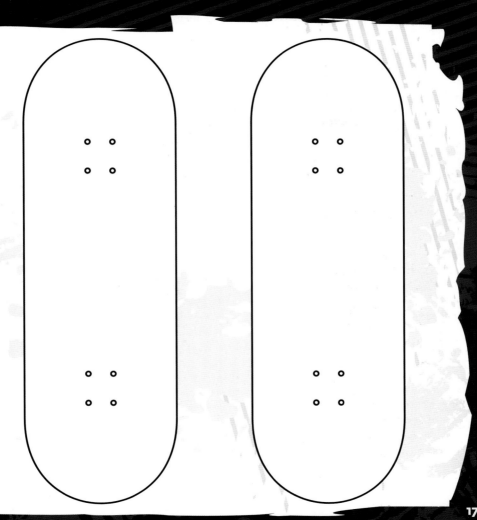

BASIC TRICKS

Start here to learn the basics.

You've got this!

SHUVIT

The Shuvit is a great first trick to learn—all you need is your board and basic finger position. Then you're ready to go!

1. Put your hand in the standard finger position: index finger in the middle of the board and middle finger on the tail.

2. Use your middle finger to push the tail of the board down and toward you, to spin the board around. Lift your index finger up slightly at the same time, to allow the board room to spin.

Tip:
This trick requires a light touch. If you push your middle finger down too hard, you'll wipe out!

3

3. When the board finishes its 180-degree spin—with the nose ending up where the tail was—place both fingers back down on the board. You did it!

POP SHUVIT

This trick takes the Shuvit to the next level! It's basically the same as a Shuvit, but you'll pop the board into the air before spinning it, and then catch it in the air. It's a harder trick, and takes a lot more practice. It's an important trick to learn when you're starting out—you'll use it in a lot of the other tricks later in the book.

1. Start in the standard finger position, and then roll the board forward.

1-2

2. Use your middle finger to push the tail of the board down hard, popping it into the air.

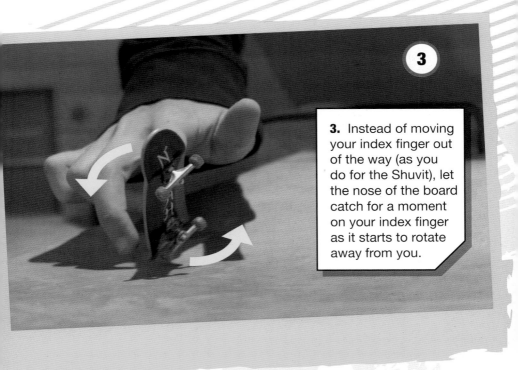

3. Instead of moving your index finger out of the way (as you do for the Shuvit), let the nose of the board catch for a moment on your index finger as it starts to rotate away from you.

Keep reading about the Pop Shuvit on the next page!

4

4. Then move your entire hand slightly away from the board to let it finish rotating 180 degrees.

5. When the board has made its full 180-degree spin, catch it in the air with both fingers, land it on the ground, and roll away.

OLLIE

The Ollie is the most important beginner trick! Once you can Ollie, you can start learning pretty much every other trick on a fingerboard. There's no such thing as practicing Ollies too much—it's truly a fundamental move to know.

1

2. Push your middle finger down hard on the tail while snapping your wrist to pop the board into the air.

1. Start in the standard finger position and roll the board forward.

2

3. At the same time, slide your index finger toward the middle of the nose to level the board out. This prevents the board from flipping backward, and the friction of your index finger actually helps lift the back end of the board.

Keep reading about the Ollie on the next page!

4. Once your board reaches the peak of its arc through the air, keep both fingers on the board, and float it back to the ground.

4

Beginners have several ways to practice the motions of an Ollie. It's a delicate move and tricky to master, so don't get discouraged if you're having trouble at first. Stay with it—you'll get it!

Practice popping in place:

You can practice just popping your board in place to help you really get the form of this move down. You might try popping your board on a pillow or other soft surface to help spring it upward more easily.

Keep reading about the Ollie on the next page!

Practice on your leg or arm:

Try using your arm or leg (for example, the side of your thigh) as a riding surface. Doing this allows you to lean the board back until it's vertical, or even tilted backward, making it easier to lift the board upward with your index finger. This eliminates the need for you to pop the board, so you can focus on getting the hand motions down.

Practice on a ramp:

Using the same technique as practicing on your leg, you can practice Ollies on vert ramps (like a half-pipe or quarter-pipe), going up the ramp as you Ollie. That will let you pull the board back enough to lift it into the air more easily.

Practice on a flat surface with obstacles:

Once you can Ollie on your leg or a ramp consistently, you know the basic form of the move. Try moving to a flat surface, like a table, and placing an obstacle in your board's path. Even household objects can work as obstacles! Then practice your Ollie. The obstacle will force you to pop the board high enough to get over it. You can build the height of your Ollie by increasing the height of obstacles!

NOLLIE

The Nollie is just like the Ollie, but you'll pop into the air from the nose instead of from the tail. It's the same motion as an Ollie, but with your fingers reversed!

1. Instead of the standard finger position, place your index finger up on the nose of your board and your middle finger in the center of the board.

2. Start skating forward, then pop the nose of the board down with your index finger.

Keep reading about the Nollie on the next page!

3. As the board pops up, slide your middle finger toward the tail to level the board out.

(4)

4. Once your board reaches the peak of its arc through the air, keep both fingers on the board, and float it back to the ground.

Tip:
Make sure you've built up some speed and momentum as you get ready to perform this trick!

MANUAL

The Manual is a simple trick that looks stylish and can be performed before and after Ollies and flip tricks to pull off advanced lines and combos! It's also known as the Manny.

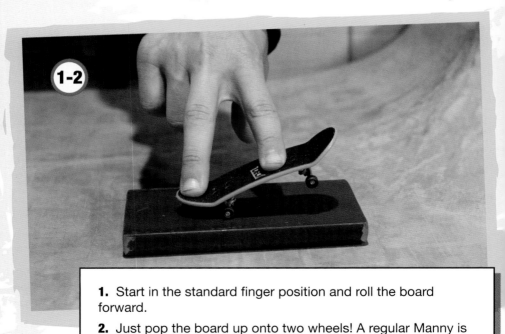

1. Start in the standard finger position and roll the board forward.

2. Just pop the board up onto two wheels! A regular Manny is done on the back wheels, so you'll press down on the tail with your middle finger.

3. Alternately, a Nose Manual is done on the front wheels—slide your index finger forward to the nose for this version.

4. Ride it out as long as you can!

INTERMEDIATE
TRICKS

Make sure you've mastered the Ollie before trying any of these killer tricks!

KICKFLIP

Flips are sick tricks that will get you some serious respect. And once you learn to Kick-flip, you'll have the basis for learning many more advanced tricks. So let's get to it!

1-2

1. Start in the standard finger position and roll the board forward.

2. Just as you'd do for a basic Ollie, pop the tail of the board down with your middle finger.

3. But—and here's where this trick is different from the Ollie—as the board lifts and you slide your index finger up to level the board, slide it up and off the side of the nose that's toward you. This will flip the board inward.

Keep reading about the the Kickflip on the next page!

(4)

4. Keep your fingers above the board, giving it enough room to flip.

5. Wait for a full rotation of the board—the wheels will turn to the sky and then turn back to the ground again. Catch the board with your fingers to stop the rotation, slam it to the ground, and roll away.

HEELFLIP

A Heelflip is like a Kickflip, but the board flips in the opposite direction!

1-2

1. Start in the standard finger position and roll the board forward.

2. Pop the tail of the board down with your middle finger, as you'd do for an Ollie or Kickflip.

3

3. As the board lifts and you slide your index finger up to level it out, slide it up and off the side of the nose that's away from you. This will flip the board outward.

Tip:
Tilting the board toward you before popping it can actually help you flick the board at the right angle.

4. Wait for a full rotation of the board, then catch the board with your fingers, slam it down to land, and roll away.

45

SLIDES

Slides are tricks where you perform an Ollie with a 90-degree twist and then land the underside of your board on an obstacle—a bench, a curb, a rail, a ledge, or really, the edge of anything! The bottom of the deck itself slides across the obstacle. (For Grinds, you land on one or two of your trucks instead of the board. Turn to page 52 to learn more about Grinds!)

Tip:
Keep practicing your Ollie, because the more control you have over it, the better you'll be able to position your board for any type of Slide.

Tip:
To look like a pro, try to keep the same speed throughout your whole Slide and perform it in one smooth motion!

BOARDSLIDE

For a Boardslide, use the middle of the deck to slide on. You can approach the obstacle from any angle: straight on, in front of you and your hand for a Frontside Boardslide, or in between you and your hand for a Backside Boardslide.

1. Roll toward the obstacle and launch into the air with an Ollie.

Keep reading about the Boardslide on the next page!

BOARDSLIDE

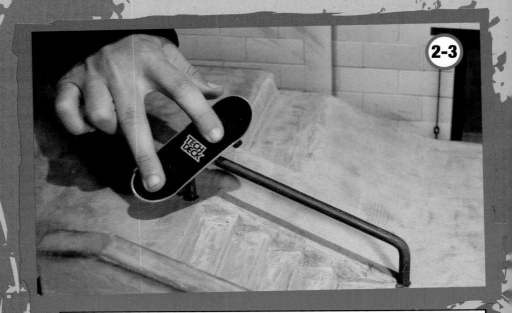

2-3

2. While you're in the air, turn the board 90 degrees so that the middle of it (in between the trucks) will land on the obstacle you'll slide on.

3. Slide your way down or across the obstacle!

4. At the end of the obstacle, put a little pressure on the back of the board to keep it level as you hop your board back to the ground and roll away.

TAILSLIDE

A Tailslide is like a Boardslide, but the slide happens on the tail of the board instead of the middle!

1

1. Roll toward the obstacle and launch into the air with an Ollie.

2-3

2. While you're in the air, turn the board so that the tail will land on the obstacle you'll slide on.

3. Slide your way down or across the obstacle!

4

4. At the end of the obstacle, hop your board back to the ground with a small pop to the tail and then roll away.

GRINDS

To Grind, land with just your trucks on any type of obstacle and coast down or across it. Depending on the type of Grind, you'll land with either one or both of your trucks.

Tip:
The better you can control your Ollie, the better you'll be able to control your Grinds.

Tip:
To look like a pro, try to keep the same speed throughout your whole Grind and perform it in one smooth motion!

50/50 GRIND

For a 50/50 Grind, you'll slide with both of your trucks flat on an obstacle such as a rail or a ledge. You can approach it straight on or from the front side or back side.

1. Roll toward the obstacle and launch into the air with an Ollie.

Keep reading about the 50/50 Grind on the next page!

2. Land with both of your trucks flat on the obstacle, and slide forward.

3. To dismount, as you approach the end of the obstacle, pop the front of your board up by pushing down slightly on the tail with your middle finger. That will let you slide off nicely and land flat on the ground. Then roll away!

ADVANCED TRICKS

Make sure you've mastered the Ollie, Pop Shuvit, and Kickflip before attempting these tricks!

VARIAL KICKFLIP

A Varial Kickflip is basically a Pop Shuvit and Kickflip combined. The deck will spin 180 degrees (as it does in a Pop Shuvit) AND flip completely around (as it does in a Kickflip) at the same time!

1. Start in the standard finger position and roll the board forward.

2. Pop the tail of the board down as you would for a Pop Shuvit.

3. Slide your index finger up and let it catch the corner of the nose just enough to make it begin flipping inward and rotating away from you.

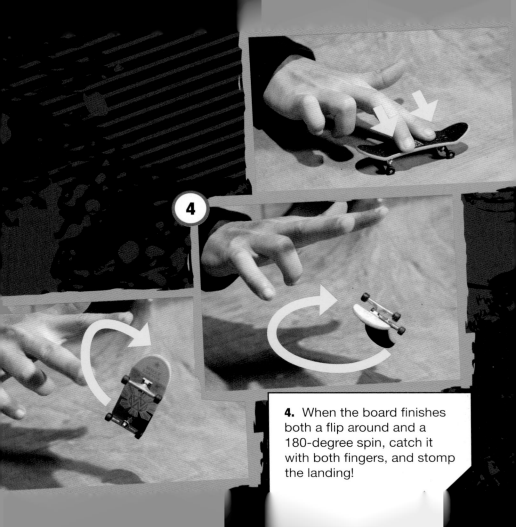

4. When the board finishes both a flip around and a 180-degree spin, catch it with both fingers, and stomp the landing!

60 FLIP

The 360 Flip, also known as a Tre Flip or Three Flip, is basically a Varial Kickflip plus another Shuvit. The deck will spin 360 degrees AND flip completely around (as it does in a Kickflip) at the same time!

1. Start in the standard finger position and roll the board forward.

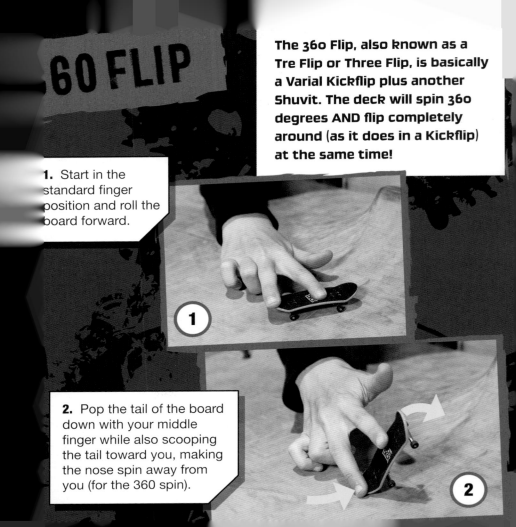

2. Pop the tail of the board down with your middle finger while also scooping the tail toward you, making the nose spin away from you (for the 360 spin).

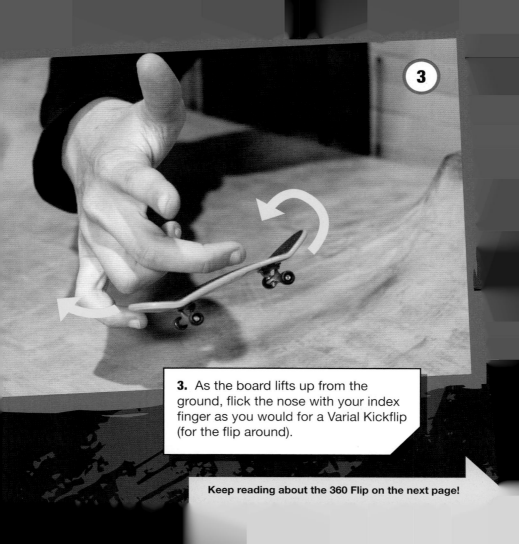

3. As the board lifts up from the ground, flick the nose with your index finger as you would for a Varial Kickflip (for the flip around).

Keep reading about the 360 Flip on the next page!

Continued

4. Keep your hand above the board, giving it enough space to rotate.